Bible Question Class Books

Bible Study Questions on
Daniel
by David E. Pratte

A workbook suitable for Bible classes, family studies, or personal Bible study

Available in print at
www.gospelway.com/sales

Bible Study Questions on Daniel:
A workbook suitable for Bible classes, family studies, or personal Bible study

© Copyright David E. Pratte, 2018
All rights reserved

ISBN-13: 978-1722698720
ISBN-10: 1722698721

Printed books, booklets, and tracts available at
www.gospelway.com/sales
Free Bible study articles online at www.gospelway.com
Free Bible courses online at www.biblestudylessons.com
Free class books at www.biblestudylessons.com/classbooks
Free commentaries on Bible books at www.biblestudylessons.com/commentary
Contact the author at www.gospelway.com/comments

Note carefully: No teaching in any of our materials is intended or should ever be construed to justify or to in any way incite or encourage personal vengeance or physical violence against any person.

"He who glories, let him glory in the Lord" – 1 Corinthians 1:31

Front Page Photo

Daniel in the Lion's Den
(artist's conception)

Then Daniel said to the king, "O king, live forever! My God sent His angel and shut the lions' mouths, so that they have not hurt me, because I was found innocent before Him; and also, O king, I have done no wrong before you." – Daniel 6:21,22 (NKJV)

Photo credit: Public domain, via Wikimedia Commons

Scripture quotations are generally from the New King James Version (NKJV), copyright 1982, 1988 by Thomas Nelson, Inc. used by permission. All rights reserved.

Other Books by the Author

Topical Bible Studies

Growing a Godly Marriage & Raising Godly Children
Why Believe in God, Jesus, and the Bible? (evidences)
The God of the Bible (study of the Father, Son, and Holy Spirit)
Grace, Faith, and Obedience: The Gospel or Calvinism?
Kingdom of Christ: Future Millennium or Present Spiritual Reign?
Do Not Sin Against the Child: Abortion, Unborn Life, & the Bible
True Words of God: Bible Inspiration and Preservation

Commentaries on Bible Books

Genesis	*Gospel of John*
Joshua and Ruth	*Acts*
Judges	*Romans*
1 Samuel	*Galatians*
2 Samuel	*Ephesians*
Ezra, Nehemiah, and Esther	*Philippians and Colossians*
Job	*Hebrews*
Proverbs	*James and Jude*
Gospel of Mark	*1 & 2 Peter*
	1,2,3 John

Bible Question Class Books

Genesis	*Gospel of Mark*
Joshua and Ruth	*Gospel of Luke*
Judges	*Gospel of John*
1 Samuel	*Acts*
2 Samuel	*Romans*
Ezra, Nehemiah, and Esther	*1 Corinthians*
Job	*2 Corinthians and Galatians*
Proverbs	*Ephesians and Philippians*
Ecclesiastes	*Colossians, 1&2 Thessalonians*
Isaiah	*1 & 2 Timothy, Titus, Philemon*
Daniel	*Hebrews*
Gospel of Matthew	*General Epistles (James - Jude)*
	Revelation

Workbooks with Study Notes

Jesus Is Lord: Workbook on the Fundamentals of the Gospel of Christ
Following Jesus: Workbook on Discipleship
God's Eternal Purpose in Christ: Workbook on the Theme of the Bible
Family Reading Booklist

Visit our website at www.gospelway.com/sales to see a current list of books in print.

Bible Study Questions on Daniel

Note: Prophecies in Daniel 7-12 make a very challenging study. Please enter the study of Daniel only if you are willing to deal with some deep, challenging material.

Introduction:

This workbook was designed for Bible class study, family study, or personal study. The class book is suitable for teens and up. The questions contain minimal human commentary, but instead urge students to study to understand Scripture.

Enough questions are included for teachers to assign as many questions as they want for each study session. Studies may proceed at whatever speed and depth will best accomplish the needs of the students.

Questions labeled "think" are intended to encourage students to apply what they have learned. When questions refer to a map, students should consult maps in a Bible dictionary or similar reference work or in the back of their Bibles. (Note: My abbreviation "*b/c/v*" means "book, chapter, and verse.")

For class instruction, I urge teachers to assign the questions as homework so students come to class prepared. Then let class time consist of **discussion** that focuses on the Scriptures themselves. Let the teacher use other Scriptures, questions, applications, and comments to promote productive discussion, not just reading the questions to see whether they were answered "correctly." Please, do *not* let the class period consist primarily of the following: "Joe, will you answer number 1?" "Sue, what about number 2?" Etc.

I also urge students to emphasize the **Bible** teaching. Please, do not become bogged down over "What did the author mean by question #5?" My meaning is relatively unimportant. The issue is what the Bible says. Concentrate on the meaning and applications of Scripture. If a question helps promote Bible understanding, stay with it. If it becomes unproductive, move on.

The questions are not intended just to help students understand the Scriptures. They are also designed to help students learn good principles of Bible study. Good Bible study requires defining the meaning of keywords, studying parallel passages, explaining the meaning of the text clearly, making applications, and defending the truth as well as exposing religious error. I have included questions to encourage students to practice all these study principles.

Note that some questions on this book are more difficult and advanced. The study leader may want to skip some questions if he/she is teaching a less advanced study.

Finally, I encourage plain applications of the principles studied. God's word is written so souls may please God and have eternal life. Please study it with the respect and devotion it deserves!

For whatever good this material achieves, to God be the glory.

Bible study commentary and notes to accompany some of our workbooks are available at www.gospelway.com/sales

© David E. Pratte, July 17, 2018

Workbooks, commentaries, and topical studies for sale in print at www.gospelway.com/sales
To join our mailing list to be informed of new books or special sales, contact the author at www.gospelway.com/comments

Assignments on Daniel 1

Please read the book of Daniel and answer the following questions on chapter 1.

1. For each of the following passages, summarize what it tells us about Daniel:

Ezekiel 14:14,20 –

Ezekiel 28:3 –

Matthew 24:15 –

2. In your own words state the theme of the book.

3. Summarize briefly the life of Daniel.

4. Describe some historical background of the book. What other prophets lived during this time? (Bible dictionaries may help.)

> 5. **Special Assignment:** Research the apocryphal sections of the book of Daniel and summarize what you learn about them. What evidence is there for accepting or not accepting them as Scripture?

6. Describe how Daniel's story begins – 1:1,2. (Find Babylon on a *map*.)

7. Explain the background that tells why Judah went into captivity – 2 Kings 23:28-37.

8. What plan did the king have for young men – 1:3,4? What kind of men were chosen? (Think: What does this tell you about Daniel?)

9. Describe the training they were to be given – 1:5.

10. What young men were chosen, and what names were they given – 1:6,7?

11. What decision did Daniel make in 1:8? (Think: What reasons might have motivated Daniel to make this choice?)

12. **Application**: What qualities does this event show Daniel possessed?

13. What objection did the chief of the eunuchs raise to Daniel's concern – 1:10?

14. What did Daniel propose as a test – 1:11-13?

15. **Application**: Explain how Daniel's approach to the problem demonstrated wisdom. What can we learn about dealing with the problems that we face?

16. What was the result of the test – 1:14,15?

17. What did the chief of the eunuchs agree to do as a result – 1:16?

18. What qualities did Daniel and his friends develop – 1:17? Who was the source of these qualities? (Think: What should we learn about our blessings?)

19. What did the king discover when he examined Daniel and his friends – 1:18-20?

20. **Application**: What lessons should young people learn from Daniel and his friends?

Workbook on Daniel

Assignments on Daniel 2

Please read Daniel chapter 2 and answer the following questions.

1. Who had a dream? When was it, and what effect did it have on him – 2:1?

2. Whom did he call to him about the dream – 2:2? What kind of practices would these men have been involved in?

3. What concern did the king express, and what offer did the men whom he had called make – 2:3,4?

4. What consequences did the king offer for those who could not interpret his dream, and what were the consequences for those who could interpret it – 2:5,6?

5. What request did the men repeat, and what demand did the king continue to make – 2:7-9? What reason did he give for doing this his way?

6. **Application**: Explain why Nebuchadnezzar's approach was wise. How was it a good test? What can we learn about testing those today who claim supernatural powers?

7. Why did the king's advisors say they could not answer his request – 2:10,11?

8. **Application**: What did the wise men's answer reveal about their power? How does this help us understand the nature of true direct revelation?

9. What command did the king give then about the advisors – 2:12?

10. How was the king's command a problem for Daniel and his friends – 2:13?

11. Who was Arioch, and what was his responsibility – 2:14?

12. What question did Daniel ask, and what request did he make – 2:15,16?

13. How did Daniel and his friends request help in answering the king's request – 2:17,18?

14. When and how was the answer given – 2:19?

15. **Special Assignment**: List other Bible examples in which true prophets were willing to confront false prophets and demonstrate their superior power from God.

16. How did Daniel respond to the fact that God had answered his prayer – 2:20? What should we learn?

17. What powers did Daniel say God has in 2:21? Explain each of these powers and give examples that illustrate these powers.

18. What powers did Daniel say God has in 2:22? How does this relate to the request that Daniel made?

19. What did Daniel say God had done in 2:23?

20. What did Daniel do when he had received this information from God – 2:24?

21. When Daniel was brought before the king, what did the king ask – 2:25,26?

22. How did Daniel contrast God's power to that of the occult advisors – 2:27,28?

23. **Special Assignment:** List other examples in which sorcerers, magicians, or other occult practitioners failed compared to the power of God.

24. **Application**: List other **passages** that warn about the dangers of the occult (sorcerers, witches, magicians, etc.). Explain what the Bible teaches.

25. What did Daniel say was the purpose of the king's dreams – 2:28,29?

26. What did Daniel explain about the source of knowledge he had – 2:30? What should we learn?

27. What did Daniel say the king saw in his dream – 2:31? How did he describe it?

28. List the parts of the image and state what each part was made of – 2:32,33.

29. What happened to the image? What happened to the stone that struck it – 2:34,35?

30. To what did the head of gold refer in the interpretation – 2:36-38?

31. How did Daniel describe Nebuchadnezzar's kingdom?

32. To what did the next two sections of the image refer – 2:39? How are they described?

33. What was the next part of the image and how is it described – 2:40?

> 34. **Special Assignment:** Each of the four parts of the image represents something clearly identifiable in history (all are mentioned elsewhere in Scripture). Consider the following: What word is used to refer to each of the four parts? How many are there? How large or influential are they? Identify what each part of the image represents.

35. How are the feet and toes described, and what does this represent – 2:41-43? (Think: Is this a separate kingdom or just part of the fourth kingdom?)

36. What would God set up, and how is it described – 2:44?

37. When would this kingdom be set up? (Think: How can identifying the fourth kingdom prove to us when God's kingdom would be established?)

38. What would the stone do to the other kingdoms – 2:45?

39. How did Nebuchadnezzar react to Daniel's interpretation of the dream – 2:46,47?

40. What effect did these events have on Daniel and his friends – 2:48,49?

Workbook on Daniel

41. Explain what each scripture below teaches about the beginning of Jesus' kingdom.
Mark 1:14,15 –

Mark 9:1 –

Acts 1:3-8 –

Acts 2:1-4,29-33 –

42. What does each of the following scriptures teach about whether Jesus kingdom is an earthly kingdom or spiritual in nature?
Matthew 16:18,19 –

John 18:36 –

Colossians 1:13,14 –

43. Explain what each of the following scriptures says about whether or not Jesus' kingdom exists today.
1 Corinthians 15:24-26 –

Colossians 1:13,14 –

Hebrews 12:28 –

Revelation 1:9 –

44. **Special Assignment:** Based on these studies, what do you conclude about the origin and nature of Jesus' kingdom? When did it begin, and does it exist today?

45. **Case Study:** Premillennialism says Jesus came to establish His kingdom during the Roman Empire, but He failed because the Jews rejected Him. So He must establish an earthly kingdom when He returns. Based on what we have studied, how would you respond?

Assignments on Daniel 3

Please read Daniel chapter 3 and answer the following questions.

1. What did Nebuchadnezzar make – 3:1? How large was it? Where did he put it?

2. Whom did he call together and for what purpose – 3:2?

3. List other **passages** about the dangers of idolatry.

> 4. **Special Assignment:** Describe the differences between idolatry and worship of the true God.

> 5. **Application:** What are some ways people today are guilty of idolatry?

> 6. **Special Assignment:** What is the attraction of idolatry? Why do people want to worship idols? Why would Nebuchadnezzar worship an idol after praising God in chapter 2?

7. What were the people who attended the dedication required to do – 3:3-5?

8. What was the penalty for refusing – 3:6.7?

> 9. **Application**: How does this contrast to the true purpose of government?

10. Who had a problem as a result, and what accusation was made – 3:8-12?

Workbook on Daniel

11. How did the king react to the accusation – 3:13-15? What threat did he make?

12. **Special Assignment:** What challenge did Nebuchadnezzar make to God? Why might he say such a thing?

13. What claim did Daniel's three friends make about God – 3:16,17?

14. What intention did they state regardless of God's deliverance – 3:18?

15. **Special Assignment:** Were the friends sure God would save them? Does God always deliver His people from persecution? Give examples.

16. **Application**: What does the Bible teach about subjection to rulers? Were the friends right to disobey the king? Explain and give Scripture for your answer.

17. **Application**: List examples of dangers we may face today that require courage like that shown by Daniel's friends.

18. What command did the king give then – 3:19-21?

19. What extra measures were taken to make sure the men would be punished?

20. What happened to the men who threw the three friends into the furnace – 3:22,23?

Page #13   *Workbook on Daniel*

21. **Special Assignment:** Summarize the evidence from the story that shows that survival would have been impossible by natural law.

22. What question did the king ask, and what did he say that he saw – 3:24,25? (Think: What is the significance of the fact there was a fourth person in the furnace?)

23. What command did the king give then – 3:26?

24. Describe what was observed when the friends came out from the furnace – 3:27.

25. **Application**: Explain how the story demonstrates the nature of true miracles.

26. **Case Study:** How does this event compare to claims made by people who claim to be able to do miracles today?

27. What conclusion did the king reach about Daniel's friends and their God – 3:28?

28. What decree did he make – 3:29?

29. **Application**: What should we learn about the purpose of true miracles?

30. What did the king do in the end for Daniel's friends – 3:30?

Workbook on Daniel   Page #14

Assignments on Daniel 4

Please read Daniel chapter 4 and answer the following questions.

1. Whose message is recorded in chapter 4? To whom was it addressed – 4:1?

2. What was the purpose of his message – 4:2?

3. How did he describe God in 4:3? (Think: Does this mean that Nebuchadnezzar had come to believe in God as the one true God?)

> 4. **Special Assignment:** Consider Nebuchadnezzar's history and explain why it was important for God to teach him the lessons discussed in this chapter.

5. What happened to Nebuchadnezzar, and how did he react – 4:4,5?

6. Whom did he call and what request did he make – 4:6,7? What was the result? (Think: Of what previous event does this remind us?)

7. Who was called next? Why did Nebuchadnezzar have confidence in him – 4:8,9?

8. What did Nebuchadnezzar see in his dream, and how did he describe it – 4:10-12? (Think: Could this be a literal tree? Explain.)

9. What did he see next, and what instruction was given about the tree – 4:13,14?

10. What was left of the tree, and what happened to it – 4:15?

11. What happened then – 4:16? How long did this last?

> 12. **Special Assignment:** What would be the difference between the heart of a man and the heart of an animal? How does this help us understand at this point that the vision is not really about a literal tree?

13. What would be the purpose of this event – 4:17,18?

14. How did Daniel first react when he heard the dream – 4:19? What reason did he give for this reaction? Explain.

15. What was the symbolic meaning of the tree – 4:20-22? Explain the similarity.

16. What did Daniel say was the significance of what happened to the tree – 4:23-25? (Think: Consider the significance of the seven times.)

17. Why was the stump of the tree left in the ground – 4:26?

18. What advice did Daniel give to Nebuchadnezzar based on the dream – 4:27? (Think: What does this show about Nebuchadnezzar?)

19. When was the dream fulfilled, and what was Nebuchadnezzar doing – 4:28,29?

20. What did Nebuchadnezzar say – 4:30? (Think: Why might a great ruler like Nebuchadnezzar be tempted to say things like this?)

> 21. **Special Assignment:** What did this show about why he needed the lesson that the dream predicted – 4:30?

22. What happened as Nebuchadnezzar spoke that brought about the fulfillment of the dream – 4:31,32?

23. Describe the circumstances that then came upon Nebuchadnezzar – 4:33.

> 24. **Special Assignment:** How would these circumstances be a great change for a man like Nebuchadnezzar? What effect would such an event tend to have on him?

25. What happened to Nebuchadnezzar at the end of the time – 4:34?

26. What did Nebuchadnezzar then understand about the nature of God?

27. List other *passages* about the eternal nature of God.

28. What did Nebuchadnezzar learn about the power of God – 4:35?

29. List other *passages* about the power of God.

Page #17   Workbook on Daniel

> 30. **Application**: Based on the lessons Nebuchadnezzar learned, what can we conclude about the true God as compared to idols?

31. What happened to the king after he learned these lessons – 4:36?

32. How did he describe God at the end – 4:37?

> 33. **Special Assignment:** List and explain other **passages** about the proper role of government.

> 34. **Application**: What lessons should rulers today learn from these events?

35. Give examples that show that rulers today often have the same problems that Nebuchadnezzar had.

> 36. **Application**: What lessons should we as citizens learn?

37. Explain how the lessons of the chapter can help us especially in times of government corruption and wickedness.

Assignments on Daniel 5

Please read Daniel chapter 5 and answer the following questions.

1. Who was king of Babylon at this time – 5:1? How and with whom did he celebrate?

2. What did he use in the celebration – 5:2,3? How had they obtained these vessels? (Think: How does this illustrate the way that pagan rulers often celebrated?)

3. **Special Assignment:** "Scholars" in past years claimed Babylon had no king named Belshazzar, so the Bible was wrong. Search what sources you may have (Bible dictionaries, etc.) to see what you can learn about Belshazzar and his relationship to Nebuchadnezzar.

4. Explain how Belshazzar's error was similar to that of Nebuchadnezzar in chapter 4.

5. **Application**: Give examples in which people today take things that God intended to be used in His spiritual service, but people use them in secular or unspiritual ways.

6. What did the people do that would especially offend God – 5:4?

7. What appeared in the sight of the king, and what did it do – 5:5?

8. What effect did this have on Belshazzar – 5:6?

9. Whom did Belshazzar call, and what did he offer them – 5:7?

10. What events earlier in the book involve similar requests?

> **11. Special Assignment:** A search to see why Belshazzar offered the third position in the kingdom (rather than the second) can lead to interesting facts. See what you can find.

12. What results did the wise men achieve and how did this affect the rulers – 5:8,9?

13. Who came to offer help, and whom did she say should be called – 5:10-12?

14. How did she describe Daniel and his abilities?

15. When the king called Daniel, what did he say he had heard about him – 5:13,14?

16. What offer did he make did Daniel – 5:15,16?

17. What did Daniel say about the king's rewards, but what did he offer to do – 5:17?

> **18. Application**: Is it acceptable for teachers and preachers of God's word to be financially supported (give Scripture)? (Think: Why might Daniel not want the rewards?)

19. How did Daniel describe king Nebuchadnezzar – 5:18,19?

20. What did Daniel say happened to Nebuchadnezzar, and for what purpose – 5:20,21?

Workbook on Daniel   Page #20

21. How did Daniel describe Belshazzar's error – 5:22,23?

22. How did Daniel describe the gods that Belshazzar worshiped?

23. By way of contrast, how did Daniel describe the true God?

24. **Application**: What lessons should we learn about the difference between the true God and false gods?

25. List each of the words that the hand sent by God had written on the wall and explain the significance of each one – 5:24-28.

26. What lesson was the message intended to teach Belshazzar?

27. What reward did Belshazzar give to Daniel – 5:29?

28. How was the message written on the wall fulfilled – 5:30,31?

29. **Special Assignment:** See what you can learn about Babylon's fall to the Persians.

30. **Application**: What other lessons can we learn about Daniel as a prophet and his message to Belshazzar?

Assignments on Daniel 6

Please read Daniel chapter 6 and answer the following questions.

1. Who became ruler after the fall of Babylon? How did he organize the kingdom – 6:1? What kingdom was this?

2. What position was Daniel given – 6:2?

3. What position did the king consider giving Daniel – 6:3? Why?

> 4. ***Special Assignment:*** In what ways was Daniel like Joseph? What lessons should we learn?

5. What attitude did other leaders take toward Daniel – 6:4? Why did their efforts fail?

> 6. ***Application***: What lessons should we learn about the attitudes people often have toward the successes of others? How should we deal with such attitudes?

7. In what aspect of Daniel's life did the men seek to entrap him – 6:5?

> 8. ***Application***: Daniel's faithfulness to the Lord was so well known that even his enemies knew he would not compromise it. What should we learn for our lives?

9. What decree did the enemies ask the king to make – 6:6,7?

10. In what way did the enemies mislead the king to get him to make the decree?

11. What aspect of law was important to the plot – 6:8,9?

12. **Special Assignment:** Explain how these enemies intended for this plot to lead to Daniel's downfall.

13. What practice of Daniel was important to the plot – 6:10?

14. What did Daniel do when he heard that the decree had been made?

15. **Application**: What lessons can we learn from Daniel about prayer and about the practice of prayer in our own lives?

16. List other *passages* about the importance of prayer.

17. How did Daniel's enemies proceed to catch him – 6:11?

18. What accusation did the enemies then make before the king – 6:12,13?

19. How did the king react when he heard the accusation – 6:14?

> 20. **Special Assignment:** What does the king's reaction show us about him? What lessons should we learn from the mistake that he made?

21. What reminder did the enemies make to the king – 6:15?

22. What did the king finally do to Daniel, and what reassurance did he express – 6:16?

23. Explain the significance of the king's official action in 6:17.

24. How did the king spend the night while Daniel was in the lion's den – 6:18? What does this show about the king?

25. What did the king do very early in the morning – 6:19,20?

26. What did Daniel say had happened – 6:21,22? What reason did he give why God had protected him?

27. How is Daniel's condition described when he came from the den – 6:23? What reason is given why Daniel was spared?

> 28. **Application**: What lessons should we learn about the conditions we must meet in prayer in order for God to answer?

29. List other **passages** showing conditions we must meet for God to answer prayer.

30. What new command did the king give then – 6:24? Why would the king give such a command?

31. What happened when these people were cast into the den of lions?

32. **Special Assignment:** List the aspects of this event that demonstrate that Daniel's deliverance was miraculous.

33. **Special Assignment:** Explain how this helps demonstrate the nature of true Bible miracles in contrast to what some people today claim to be miracles.

34. What decree did the king make then – 6:25,26?

35. List the characteristics that the king said God possesses – 6:26,27.

36. Explain how these events would have led the king to these conclusions.

37. **Special Assignment:** Explain how this event demonstrates the purpose of miracles.

38. What was the final outcome described regarding Daniel – 6:28?

39. **Application**: Explain how this event demonstrated the faith of Daniel, and explain lessons that we should learn.

Assignments on Daniel 7

Please read Daniel chapter 7 and answer the following questions.

1. Look over the last six chapters of Daniel and describe how these chapters fundamentally differ from the first six chapters. (Note: Due to the prophetic nature of these chapters, we will often wait till we have a full description before attempting explanations.)

2. How was the message in chapter 7 presented to Daniel – 7:1? When did this happen? Where was he?

3. What did he see according to 7:2,3?

4. **Special Assignment:** What would winds and sea represent in symbolic, prophetic language? Consider these examples: Isaiah 17:12; 57:20; Revelation 13:1; 17:15; 20:13; 21:1; Jeremiah 49:32,36; 51:1.

5. **Case Study:** Daniel's revelations are so specific and accurate that skeptics deny they were written till centuries after the Babylonian and Persian empires ended. Explain the significance in this regard of the fact Daniel gives specific times when the visions occurred. What is the correct explanation for the accuracy of the prophecies?

6. Describe each of the beasts that Daniel saw in the following verses:

7:4 –

7:5 –

7:6 –

7:7 –

7. Describe the horns that appeared in the vision of the fourth beast – 7:8. What happened to them?

Workbook on Daniel

> 8. **Special Assignment:** Are the animals that are described literal or symbolic? Explain how you know.

9. Who appears in 7:9? How is He described?

10. What term is used to name Him? Whom does this describe? Explain the significance of the term.

11. List other **passages** in which Bible writers attempt to describe symbolically the appearance of God.

12. What further information describes the Ancient of Days in 7:10?

13. What would be the significance of a fiery stream coming from God?

14. What is the significance of books being opened? List other similar **passages**.

15. What judgment came upon the fourth beast and its horn – 7:11?

16. What happened to the other beasts – 7:12? How did this differ from the fourth beast?

17. Who then came before the Ancient of Days – 7:13? How is His coming described?

> 18. **Special Assignment:** To whom does this refer? How does this fit with Acts 1:9-11?

19. What did He receive – 7:14? How is it described? (Think: Was the kingdom given to the Son of Man when He came to God or when He left God to return to earth, as some teach?)

20. Explain how other passages help us understand what Daniel is predicting. Specifically, consider Revelation 5:6-14; Daniel 2:44; Isaiah 9:7; Luke 1:33; Hebrews 12:28.

21. How did the visions affect Daniel – 7:15,16? What request did he make? (Think: What can we learn from the fact Daniel received a revelation he did not understand?)

22. What did the four beasts represent – 7:17? (Note: Remember that references to kings in Daniel's prophecies often referred to kingdoms, not just individual rulers – see verse 23.)

> 23. **Special Assignment:** Compare the four beasts in Daniel 7 to the four parts of the image in Daniel 2. What kingdoms are represented by the four beasts?

24. What additional information is given in 7:18 about God's kingdom? What does this tell us about when God's people could enter this kingdom?

25. How is the fourth beast of Daniel 7 similar to the beast of Revelation 13?

26. What did Daniel specifically want to understand then – 7:19,20?

27. What did the horn in the fourth beast do in 7:21?

28. How long did this last, and what was the result – 7:22?

29. What does the fourth beast represent, and what will it be like – 7:23?

30. If the beasts represent kingdoms, what do the horns represent – 7:24? What would one horn do to the others? (Note: Remember the numbers are symbolic.)

> 31. **Case Study:** It is generally agreed that the fourth kingdom is the Roman Empire, and Jesus came to establish His kingdom during the Roman Empire. Many premillennialists say He failed to establish His kingdom then, so the ten horns represent ten kingdoms that will exist when He returns to establish His kingdom. How would you respond?

32. What would the horn/king do according to 7:25?

33. What would happen to him – 7:26?

> 34. **Special Assignment:** Explain similarities between Daniel's prophecy here and Revelation 13. How does this help explain Revelation 13?

35. Time. times, and half a time equals 3½ times. If a "time" refers to a year, how is this similar to Revelation 11:2,3; 12:6; 13:5 (note 3½ years = 42 months = 1260 days if each month equals 30 days). What do these time periods represent? (Remember the numbers are symbolic.)

36. What kingdom is described again in 7:27, and what happens to it? (Note: To understand the fulfillment of the prophecy and the references to the kingdom, review the Scriptures regarding the fulfillment of the vision in Daniel chapter 2.)

37. How was Daniel affected by the things revealed to him – 7:28?

Assignments on Daniel 8

Please read Daniel chapter 8 and answer the following questions.
1. When did the vision in this chapter occur – 8:1?

2. Where did Daniel see himself in the vision (see a *map*) – 8:2? (Think: What does the Bible tell us elsewhere about this place?)

3. Describe the animal that Daniel saw – 8:3.

4. What did this animal do – 8:4?

5. Describe the animal Daniel saw next – 8:5.

6. What did this second animal do to the animal that Daniel had seen first – 8:6,7? (Think: What had animals and horns represented in the previous vision?)

7. What happened when the male goat grew strong – 8:8?

8. What happened with one of its horns – 8:9?

9. What did this horn do – 8:10? (Think: For the significance of the stars in prophecy, see Joel 2:10; 3:15; Isaiah 13:10.)

10. How high did he exalt himself, and what did he do then – 8:11,12?

Workbook on Daniel

11. What question was asked in 8:13?

12. What answer was given? What would happen at the end of that time – 8:14?

13. What did Daniel want to know – 8:15? What did the one who stood before him look like? (Think: What does this tell us about how angels sometimes appeared?)

14. What instruction was given, and to whom was it given – 8:16?

15. What can we learn about this angel from other passages?

16. What did Daniel do when this one approached – 8:17? To what time did the vision refer?

17. What was Daniel doing, and what did the angel do to him – 8:18?

18. What did the angel explain about the time to which the vision applied – 8:19?

19. What explanation is given for the ram with two horns – 8:20?

20. What was the explanation for the male goat and its large horn – 8:21?

21. **Special Assignment:** Research and determine whom this large horn represented in history and when and where this conflict occurred. (Bible dictionaries or commentaries may be helpful here.)

22. What was meant by the horn that broke and four horns took its place – 8:22?

23. **Special Assignment:** Again research and determine how this was fulfilled.

24. **Special Assignment:** In the dreams and visions of Daniel 2 and 7, four kingdoms are described, but only the first one was named. How does the information here help us identify two other kingdoms?

25. 8:23 describes further the little horn of 8:9-12. What more do we learn here?

26. What harm would he cause – 8:24?

27. How high would he exalt himself, and how is his downfall described – 8:25?

28. **Special Assignment:** Again, what king in history fulfilled this prophecy? What did he do that is described here prophetically? How long did the persecution last?

29. What was Daniel told about when the vision would be fulfilled – 8:26?

30. How was Daniel affected by this information – 8:27?

Workbook on Daniel

Assignments on Daniel 9

Please read Daniel chapter 9 and answer the following questions.

1. When did the events recorded in this chapter occur – 9:1?

2. What did Daniel realize, and how did he realize it – 9:2?

3. List **passages** where this prophecy of Jeremiah may be found.

4. What did Daniel do – 9:3? (Think: What is the significance of the fasting, sackcloth, and ashes?)

5. How did he describe God in his prayer – 9:4?

6. What confession did Daniel make – 9:5?

7. Why was this confession important? See Leviticus 26:40-42; 1 Kings 8:47-49; Nehemiah chapter 9.

8. How had the people treated the prophets – 9:6?

9. How did the people's conduct compare to that of God – 9:7,8?

10. What groups of people had been guilty of sin?

11. What had been the consequence of the sins?

12. How is the conduct of the people compared to the character of God in 9:9?

13. How had the people acted, and what consequence had come upon them according to 9:10,11?

14. List other **passages** in which God had warned the people that their sins would lead to these consequences.

15. How are the consequences to the people described in 9:12?

16. Despite these consequences, what had the people failed to do – 9:13?

17. What conclusion did Daniel reach about God in 9:14? (Think: What lessons should we learn about our own lives?)

18. What had God done for the people in the past – 9:15? Yet how had the people responded to God's goodness?

19. So what was Daniel requesting God to do now – 9:16,17?

20. ***Special Assignment:*** Explain the connection between Daniel's request and the prophecies of Jeremiah (verse 2) and God's deliverance of the people from Egypt (verse 15).

21. What reason did Daniel give why he believed God should act as Daniel was requesting Him to act – 9:18,19. (Think: What should we learn about our own requests to God?)

22. ***Special Assignment:*** Summarize in your own words the purpose of Daniel's prayer.

23. Who came as Daniel was praying – 9:20,21? Where have we already read about him?

24. How did he come, and when did he come?

25. For what purpose did he come – 9:22,23?

26. What reason did he give why this information was given to Daniel?

Workbook on Daniel

27. According to 9:24, what time period had been determined, and what things would happen during that time?

28. What time period is described in 9:25? At what event would it begin, and at what event would it end? (Note: We encourage you to avoid premillennial speculations on these verses. For a Scriptural review of premillennial teaching, please study our free articles on our Bible study web site at www.gospelway.com/instruct – see the section about "Man").

29. What is meant by "your people and your holy city"?

30. What is meant by "the command to restore and build Jerusalem"? (Think: How did this relate to Daniel and his prayer?)

31. Under what circumstances would Jerusalem be restored according to 9:25?

32. **Special Assignment:** List other *scriptures* that describe the rebuilding of Jerusalem. Summarize some of the people and events involved.

33. Who fulfilled the reference to Messiah the Prince?

34. **Special Assignment:** What is meant by "to finish the transgression, to make an end of sins, to make reconciliation for iniquity, to bring in everlasting righteousness"? Explain how the Messiah accomplished these things.

35. List **passages** showing that the Messiah accomplished these things when He came. (Note Acts 3:21-24.)

36. **Special Assignment:** In what sense was the Messiah referred to as the "Holy One" or "Most Holy"? In what sense was He anointed?

37. List **passages** showing that Christ was the Holy One and that He held offices that required anointing.

38. What would happen to the Messiah after the sixty-two-week period – 9:26? Explain "not for Himself" (see Isaiah 53).

39. What is the significance of the city and the sanctuary that would be destroyed? What people of what prince accomplished this?

40. How did this involve abominations and desolation? (See Jesus' prophecy of the destruction of Jerusalem: Luke 21:20; Matthew 24:15; Mark 13:14.)

41. What covenant did Jesus confirm (note Acts 3:25; Galatians 3:16,17; Luke 1:2,52)? In what sense did He bring an end to sacrifice and offering?

42. The time periods are especially difficult to explain. Consider these thoughts:
    Are the numbers in prophecy meant to be literal or symbolic?

Note that 70 weeks = 7 x 10 x 7 days (1 week = 7 days). What is the symbolic significance in prophecy of the number 7 and the number 10? (Compare Matthew 18:22.)

Page #37   Workbook on Daniel

Assignments on Daniel 10

Please read Daniel chapter 10 and answer the following questions.

1. Who was king when these events occurred – 10:1? How is the message that Daniel received described?

2. What was Daniel doing when he received this vision – 10:2,3?

3. Where was Daniel and when was it that he saw the vision – 10:4?

4. Describe the garments of the man whom he saw – 10:5. (Think: What would such clothing indicate?)

5. How is the man himself described – 10:6? (Think: What other visions in the Bible involved someone with similar appearance?)

6. Why did the men who were with Daniel not see the vision like he did – 10:7? (Think: what does this tell you about the vision?)

7. How was Daniel himself affected by the man's appearance – 10:8? (Think: What other visions in the Bible had similar effects on people?)

8. What was Daniel's condition at the time, yet what did he hear – 10:9?

9. What happened then, and what effect did it have on Daniel – 10:10?

10. How did the man address Daniel in 10:11?

11. What reason did the man give for coming to Daniel – 10:12?

12. What reason did the man give why he had not come sooner – 10:13?

13. Who helped the man, and where else do we read about the one who helped him?

14. Whom did the vision concern, and what are we told about when it would be fulfilled – 10:14?

---

15. **Special Assignment:** Study the expression "latter days." To what period of time does this expression often refer? Prove your answer by Scripture (not opinion).

---

16. What did Daniel do when these words had been spoken – 10:15?

17. What reason did Daniel give why he could not speak – 10:16-18? How was he given strength to speak?

18. What reassurance did the man give, and what was the effect on Daniel – 10:19?

19. What did the man say that he was going to do – 10:20? (Note the nations that are involved in the future plans.)

20. What did he say that he would tell Daniel – 10:21?

Assignments on Daniel 11

Please read Daniel chapter 11 and answer the following questions.

Note: The vision of Daniel 10 continues in chapters 11 and 12. The fulfillment of the prophecies occurred in the period of silence between Malachi and the New Testament, so we have no inspired record of the fulfillment. We must rely on uninspired history. Please study commentaries or Bible encyclopedias or dictionaries for help. (The books of 1 and 2 Maccabees – or Machabees – are uninspired but generally reliable historically.)

1. What did the angel say he did and when did he do it – 11:1? Where else have we read about Darius the Mede?

2. How many significant rulers did the angel predict – 11:2? How did he describe them?

3. What would the fourth king do? (Note the references Persia and Greece. Consider which king of Persia attacked Greece. Note the connection to the book of Esther.)

4. Who would arise and how is he described – 11:3? (Think: Which king of Greece would this fit? See 1 Maccabees 1:1-10.)

5. What would happen to his kingdom then – 11:4? (Think: Find the fulfillment of this in the history of Greece. See also the vision in Daniel 8.)

6. What would one king do – 11:5? (Hint: The Seleucids ruled in Syria north of Palestine, and the Ptolemies ruled in Egypt south of Palestine.)

7. What attempt would be made to achieve an alliance – 11:6?

8. What would be the result of this attempt? (Think: See your sources for specifics.)

9. Who would follow the daughter of the king of the South, and what would he do – 11:7?

Workbook on Daniel

10. Describe his victory – 11:8. (Think: Find the fulfillment of this in your sources.)

11. What conflict followed – 11:9,10? (Think: See if you can find who was involved in this conflict.)

12. What battle followed, and what was the outcome – 11:11,12? (Think: Do your sources explain the fulfillment of this?)

13. What would the king of the North do then – 11:13?

14. Who would join in the battle – 11:14?

15. What would be the final outcome of the battle – 11:15,16? (Hint: This conflict resulted in a crucial battle at Paneas as described by the Jewish historian Josephus.)

16. What is the "Glorious Land," and what consequence came upon it.

17. What attempt would the king of the North pursue next – 11:17? What would result?

18. What would the king attempt then – 11:18? What would end the attempt? (Hint: Consider the outcome of the battle with the Romans at Magnesia.)

19. Where would the king turn next, and what would result – 11:19?

20. What would his successor do, and what would be the outcome – 11:20?

21. How is his successor described – 11:21?

22. What will he accomplish – 11:22? (Compare Daniel 8:9-12.)

23. How will this vile person act – 11:23,24?

24. What would he attempt next – 11:25,26?

25. What would be the outcome?

26. How would both kings act, and what would be the outcome – 11:27?

27. What would the vile person do as he returned home – 11:28? (For the fulfillment see 1 Maccabees 1:20-28.)

Workbook on Daniel

28. What happened the next time this vile person attempted to invade Egypt – 11:29,30? (Hint: Roman history records that a representative of Rome named Popilius met Antiochus near Alexandria and stopped him.)

29. What happened as this vile person returned home?

30. What specific consequences did he bring on the Jews – 11:31? (See 1 Maccabees 1:30-67.)

31. What did some people do at the time – 11:32? (This may refer to the Maccabees – see 1 Maccabees chapter 2.)

32. What happened to the people who had understanding – 11:33?

33. What beneficial effect did this have on the people of understanding – 11:35? (Hint: This most likely refers to the Maccabees.)

34. **Special Assignment:** 11:36 begins discussion of a king whose identity is difficult. It may still seem to be Antiochus, but verse 40 says the king of the South and the king of the North both fight against this king. Consider who it is as your study proceeds. (Hint: Consider Rome.)

35. How would this king treat gods and whose will would he do – 11:36,37?

36. What "god" would he serve – 11:38? (Think: How would he serve such a God?)

37. What benefits will result from this king – 11:39 (note the ESV)?

38. Who would oppose this king – 11:40? Describe their attack.

39. What would be the result?

40. What lands would he enter, and what countries would escape – 11:41?

41. What other land would not escape – 11:42?

42. What power will he have, and who will follow him – 11:43?

43. What would cause trouble for him, and how would he react – 11:44?

44. What area would be included in this domination, yet what would ultimately happen – 11:45?

45. **Special Assignment:** Consider the role of the Roman Empire and how it fits the theme of the prophecies of Daniel, including this context.

Assignments on Daniel 12

Please read Daniel chapter 12 and answer the following questions. (See the note at the beginning of the chapter 11.)

1. Who would stand up at that time, and where have we read about him before – 12:1? How is he described?

2. How severe will the troubles of that time be? Who would escape?

3. List other *passages* about those who are written in the book.

4. *Special Assignment:* Explain the similarity to Matthew 24:15-22; Mark 13:19,20; Luke 21:20-22. (Note that Daniel's prophecies are mentioned there.)

5. What would happen to "many" according to 12:2? This may sound like the final resurrection, but how does this differ from the number of people raised at the final resurrection – John 5:28,29?

6. What kind of resurrection is described in Ezekiel 37:14; Romans 6:3-8; Ephesians 2:1-6; 5:14; Colossians 2:12,13; 3:1; (see also Luke 15:24,32; Matthew 8:22; 1 Timothy 5:6)? Remember, Daniel's prophecies are symbolic.

7. How might a resurrection to shame and contempt relate to Matthew 24:10-13?

8. How are good people described in 12:3? Compare this to Matthew 5:14-16; Philippians 2:15,16; Ephesians 5:8.

9. What was Daniel told to do in 12:4? List other *passages* and explain the significance of a seal.

10. ***Case Study:*** Many have tried to use passages like this to predict the time of Jesus' second coming. What do we know about the time of that event according to 2 Peter 3:10; 1 Thessalonians 5:2,4; Matthew 24:34,35; Luke 21:34,35; 12:39,40; Revelation 3:3; 16:15; Mark 13:35?

11. What else could "the time of the end" refer to based on other information we have gathered?

12. What did Daniel see then, and what did one of them ask – 12:5,6?

13. What answer was given in response – 12:7?

14. Where else have we studied "times, time, and half a time"? See your notes there for more information.

15. Besides "times, time, and half a time" what more information is given about when these events will occur? (Note that we will be given more information as we proceed.)

16. What question did Daniel ask then, and what was he told – 12:8,9?

17. What contrast is stated in 12:10?

18. What might cause some to be purified, refined, and made white? Compare 11:35.

Workbook on Daniel   Page #46

19. What more information is given in 12:11?

20. According to our study of 8:11,12 and 11:31, what is meant by the removal of the daily sacrifices?

21. What is meant by the abomination of desolation? See Matthew 24:15; Mark 13:14; Luke 21:20. (Remember that the time period described is symbolic, not literal.)

22. Who receives a blessing according to 12:12?

23. How does the time period of 12:12 compare to 12:11?

24. **Special Assignment:** If the abomination of desolation refers to the fall of Jerusalem, what significant event which occurred sometime after that would be a blessing to God's people? (Hint: Consider the significance of Rome in Daniel's prophecies and the fall of Rome as described in the book of Revelation.)

25. How did the revelation to Daniel end – 12:13? Explain the meaning.

26. Review Daniel's life and summarize the challenges and difficulties that he faced.

27. **Application**: Can you think of any sin for which Daniel is guilty according to the book? What lessons can we learn for our own lives from the life of Daniel?

Printed books, booklets, and tracts available at
www.gospelway.com/sales
Free Bible study articles online at www.gospelway.com
Free Bible courses online at www.biblestudylessons.com
Free class books at www.biblestudylessons.com/classbooks
Free commentaries on Bible books at
www.biblestudylessons.com/commentary
Contact the author at www.gospelway.com/comments
Free e-mail Bible study newsletter at
www.gospelway.com/update_subscribe.htm

CPSIA information can be obtained
at www.ICGtesting.com
Printed in the USA
LVHW062236060322
712776LV00029B/580